SMART QUESTIONS & ANSWERS FOR TEENS TO APPRECIATE

A PRECIOUS KEEPSAKE

C. GABRIELLE PRATT

Copyright © 2022
No part of this book may be reproduced or copied without
written permission of the author/publisher.
All rights reserved.

HOW TO USE THIS BOOK

Dear Teen,

You are the owner of a keepsake workbook!

Take your time and go through it one day at a time. You can use it as a part of your personal quiet time. It is important to note what your beliefs are and the answers that you discover to the questions. In some instances, you would find it helpful to discuss certain matters with others or refer to different resources including the Bible to confirm your answers.

There are spaces available at intervals for you to ask your own questions and provide the answers about topics you are interested in.

One thing is certain, and that is, as you go through life you will have plenty of questions to answer. This book is considered an exploration and a keepsake. Some answers are very simple and there will be those that require more thought. It is strongly recommended that you use the Certificate of Completion at the back when done and celebrate. Secure the book in a special place and review it one year later. The goal is to see if your answers would have changed and this leads to greater self-awareness.

All the best as you explore your world and come up with answers.

The Editor

WHAT IS YOUR FULL NAME?

WHAT COUNTRY DO YOU LIVE IN?

DRAW THE FLAG BELOW

WHAT DO THE SYMBOLS ON YOUR COUNTRY'S FLAG REPRESENT?

_____

_____

_____

_____

_____

WRITE THE MOTTO OF YOUR COUNTRY

_____

_____

_____

_____

_____

WHAT SCHOOL DO YOU ATTEND?

_____

_____

_____

WHAT IS YOUR FAVORITE SUBJECT IN SCHOOL?

_____

_____

WHAT THREE WORDS WOULD YOU USE TO DESCRIBE YOUR NEIGHBORHOOD?

_____

_____

_____

_____

_____

IF YOU COULD ADD SOMETHING TO YOUR NEIGHBORHOOD WHAT WOULD IT BE?

_____

_____

_____

IF YOU FOUND $5 WHAT WOULD YOU DO WITH IT?

_____

_____

_____

_____

_____

IF YOU RECEIVED A GIFT OF $100 IN CASH WHAT WOULD YOU DO WITH IT?

_____

_____

_____

_____

My Question

The Answer

WHAT DO YOU LOOK FOR IN A PERSON TO BECOME YOUR FRIEND?

_____

_____

_____

_____

_____

WHO HAS THE BIGGEST INFLUENCE ON YOU IN YOUR FAMILY? HOW?

_____

_____

_____

_____

WHY IS THERE AN INCREASE IN STUDENTS FIGHTING?

_____

_____

_____

_____

_____

GIVE THREE TIPS THAT COULD HELP PREVENT STUDENTS FROM FIGHTING.

_____

_____

_____

_____

WHEN YOU ARE WITH OTHERS HOW MUCH TIME SHOULD YOU SPEND ON YOUR CELL PHONE IN THEIR MIDST?

_____

_____

_____

_____

_____

CAN YOU LIST THREE BENEFITS OF HAVING A CELL PHONE?

_____

_____

_____

_____

CAN YOU LIST THREE DISADVANTAGES IF ONE DOES NOT HAVE A CELL PHONE?

_____

_____

_____

_____

_____

_____

WHEN IS THE BEST TIME TO PUT UP A CELL PHONE AND TALK FACE TO FACE?

_____

_____

_____

_____

WHAT SHOULD A PERSON DO IF THEY RECEIVE AN EMBARRASSING PICTURE OF A FRIEND ON THEIR PHONE?

_____

_____

_____

_____

_____

_____

WHAT DO YOU DO IF YOU ARE NOT INCLUDED IN THE INVITATION TO FRIEND'S PARTY?

_____

_____

_____

_____

My Question

The Answer

WHY DO PEOPLE BECOME BORED?

_____

_____

_____

_____

WHAT CAUSES SOME PEOPLE TO GIVE UP IN LIFE?

_____

_____

_____

_____

DO YOU HAVE A FAVORITE MOVIE? WHAT IS THE NAME?

_____

_____

_____

WHAT PART OF THE MOVIE DID YOU REALLY ENJOY?

_____

_____

_____

_____

_____

Topic: Favorite Song

WHAT IS THE FIRST LINE IN YOUR FAVORITE SONG?

_____

_____

_____

_____

WHAT IS THE NAME OF THE PERSON/GROUP WHO PERFORMS IT?

_____

_____

_____

WHAT PLACE IN THE WORLD YOU WOULD LIKE TO VISIT? GIVE ONE REASON WHY?

_____

_____

_____

_____

_____

IF TWO PERSONS CAN ACCOMPANY YOU WHO WOULD THEY BE?

_____

_____

_____

Topic: Providing Encouragement

WHAT WOULD YOU SAY TO A FRIEND WHOSE CLOSE FAMILY MEMBER DIED SUDDENLY?

_____

_____

_____

_____

_____

WHAT WOULD YOU SAY TO A FRIEND WHOSE PARENT IS VERY SICK?

_____

_____

_____

_____

My Question For a Family Member

The Answer

_____

_____

_____

_____

_____

_____

_____

_____

_____

_____

_____

_____

_____

WHAT ARE YOUR HOBBIES?

_____

_____

_____

_____

_____

DESCRIBE TWO BENEFITS OF HAVING A HOBBY?

_____

_____

_____

_____

HOW OLD WILL YOU BE ON YOUR NEXT BIRTHDAY?

WHAT WOULD BE A GREAT WAY TO CELEBRATE IT?

WHEN IS A GOOD TIME TO SHARE ITEMS THAT YOU HAVE EXTRAS OF?

_____

_____

_____

_____

WHY IS IT SOMETIMES DIFFICULT TO SHARE ITEMS?

_____

_____

_____

_____

IF YOU CAN CORRECT TWO PROBLEMS IN YOUR COUNTRY WHAT WOULD THEY BE?

_____

_____

_____

_____

_____

_____

_____

WHAT CAN TEENS DO THAT CAN IMPROVE THE SITUATION?

_____

_____

_____

_____

_____

_____

_____

_____

WHAT IS YOUR FAVORITE HOLIDAY TO CELEBRATE?

_____

_____

DESCRIBE WHAT YOU LIKE TO DO AT THAT TIME?

_____

_____

My Question for a Pastor/Priest

The Answer

WHAT DO YOU BELIEVE IS AN EXCITING CAREER?
GIVE TWO REASONS FOR YOUR ANSWER.

_____

_____

_____

DESCRIBE HOW ONE USUALLY ENTERS THIS CAREER?

_____

_____

_____

_____

_____

WHAT THREE FACTS CAN YOU IDENTIFY ABOUT THE BIBLE?

_____

_____

_____

REWRITE THE WORDS FROM JOHN 1: 12 IN THE BIBLE.

_____

_____

_____

_____

_____

WHY DO SOME PEOPLE GET DRUNK? GIVE TWO REASONS.

_____

_____

_____

WHY DOES A PERSON BECOME AN ALCOHOLIC?

_____

_____

_____

_____

_____

WHAT ITEM FROM YOUR CLOSET YOU WOULD GLADLY GIVE AWAY?

_____

_____

_____

WHAT ITEM FROM YOUR CLOSET YOU WOULD
FIND DIFFICULT TO GIVE AWAY?

_____

_____

_____

_____

_____

WHEN IS IT PROPER TO SAY I AM SORRY? GIVE TWO EXAMPLES.

WHEN IS IT PROPER TO SAY THANK YOU? GIVE TWO EXAMPLES.

My Question for a Sports Coach

The Answer

_____

_____

_____

_____

_____

_____

_____

_____

_____

_____

_____

IF YOU HAD MORE THAN ENOUGH FOOD TO EAT TODAY WHAT WOULD YOU DO WITH THE EXTRAS?

_____

_____

_____

WHY DO SOME PEOPLE THROW AWAY FOOD THAT IS GOOD ENOUGH TO EAT?

_____

_____

_____

_____

Topic: Bullying

HOW WOULD YOU DEAL WITH SOMEONE WHO BULLIES YOU ONLINE?

_____

_____

_____

_____

_____

GIVE ONE REASON WHY PEOPLE BECOME BULLIES?

_____

_____

_____

_____

_____

WHY DO SOME PEOPLE SMOKE CIGARETTES?

_____

_____

_____

_____

WHAT ARE TWO GOOD HABITS TO PRACTICE
BEFORE YOU LEAVE HOME EACH DAY?

_____

_____

_____

_____

WHAT IS THE BEST THING TO DO WITH A RUMOUR?

_____

_____

_____

_____

GIVE TWO REASONS WHY PEOPLE GOSSIP?

_____

_____

_____

_____

IF YOU DO NOT HAVE THE FACTS ABOUT AN INCIDENT WHAT SHOULD YOU DO BEFORE SHARING IT?

_____

_____

_____

_____

IDENTIFY TWO SOURCES YOU CAN USE TO CHECK IF INFORMATION IS CORRECT?

_____

_____

_____

_____

My Question for a Nurse

The Answer

WHAT WOULD YOU SAY TO A FRIEND WHO DOES NOT KEEP THEIR PROMISES?

_____

_____

_____

_____

WHAT CAN YOU DO TO SHOW RESPECT TO SOMEONE WHOSE HOUSE YOU ARE VISITING?

_____

_____

_____

_____

WHAT WOULD YOU DO IF THE CASHIER GAVE YOU 3 DOLLARS IN CHANGE INSTEAD OF ONLY ONE?

_____

_____

_____

_____

WHAT WOULD YOU DO IF YOU FOUND A WALLET WITH $300 ON THE COUNTER IN A RESTAURANT'S BATHROOM?

_____

_____

_____

_____

WHY IS IT IMPORTANT TO TELL THE TRUTH?

_____

_____

_____

_____

GIVE ONE REASON WHY SOMEONE MAY NOT TELL THE TRUTH?

_____

_____

_____

_____

DO YOU KNOW THAT PROVERBS 6:16 LIST 7 THINGS THAT GOD HATES? LIST 4 OF THEM?

_____

_____

_____

_____

WHO DOES GOD LOVE ACCORDING TO JOHN 3:16? DOES THAT INCLUDE YOU?

_____

_____

_____

_____

WHEN SHOULD YOU OFFER A PERSON FORGIVENESS?

_____

_____

_____

_____

WHAT CAN HAPPEN IF SOMEONE DOES NOT FORGIVE YOU AND YOU NEED THEM TO?

_____

_____

_____

_____

My Question for a Police Officer

The Answer

HOW MANY COMMANDMENTS ARE LISTED IN EXODUS 20? LIST FIVE OF THEM.

_____

_____

_____

_____

_____

WHICH COMMANDMENT SEEMS VERY DIFFICULT FOR ADULTS TO KEEP?

_____

_____

_____

_____

CAN YOU LIST THREE WAYS A CHILD CAN
SHOW RESPECT TO THEIR PARENT?

_____

_____

_____

CAN YOU LIST THREE WAYS A PERSON CAN SHOW RESPECT TO
OTHERS WHO ARE NOT FAMILY?

_____

_____

_____

HOW LONG CAN A PERSON LIVE WITHOUT DRINKING WATER?

_____

_____

_____

WHAT PROBLEMS CAN HAPPEN WHEN A PERSON CANNOT GET CLEAN WATER? LIST TWO OF THEM.

_____

_____

_____

WHAT CAN YOU DO TO SHOW KINDNESS TO AN ANIMAL?

_____

_____

_____

GIVE TWO BENEFITS FOR HAVING A PET?

_____

_____

_____

WHAT THREE THINGS CAN A STUDENT DO TO PREPARE FOR A SCHOOL EXAM?

_____

_____

_____

WHAT CAN A STUDENT DO TO ENSURE THAT THEY ARE NOT LATE FOR SCHOOL?

_____

_____

_____

My Question for a Guidance Counselor

The Answer

List the different types of blood that exist. What is the most common type?

_____

_____

_____

WHAT IS THE MOST IMPORTANT REASON FOR DONATING BLOOD?

_____

_____

_____

CERTIFICATE OF COMPLETION
awarded to

. . . .

Has successfully completed

SMART QUESTIONS & ANSWERS

FOR TEENS TO APPRECIATE

A PRECIOUS KEEPSAKE

TOPIC INDEX

Send all comments and suggestions to
The Editor at P.O. Box SS- 5963 Nassau, Bahamas Or youthfulconnection1@gmail.com

Made in the USA
Columbia, SC
02 October 2024

43199258R00030